OUR
SUFFERINGS

PETER JEFFERY

EVANGELICAL PRESS OF WALES

© Evangelical Press of Wales, 1982
First published 1982
Reprinted 1986
Reprinted 1995
ISBN 0 900898 76 3

Cover design by Vincent McDonnell

Cover photograph: Courtesy of J. Clement

Published by the Evangelical Press of Wales
Bryntirion, Bridgend, Mid Glamorgan, CF31 4DX
Printed by Bridgend Print Centre

Contents

Introduction

PAIN, anguish, sorrow and suffering are experiences to which the Christian is not immune. In fact, he will probably have to face them more than the non-Christian, because, as well as the normal pressures and perplexities of life that confront all men, he has spiritual battles to cope with of which the unbeliever knows nothing.

The five testimonies which follow are from Christians who are all members of the same local church. This in itself provides evidence of the fact that suffering is a common problem among the people of God. In every fellowship of Christians there will be those who either have experienced great suffering or are at present going through it.

How can we cope at such times? And how can we help one another? There is no easy answer to these questions; all that this little book tries to do is to shed some biblical light into this dark area. The testimonies themselves do not offer any glib answers. The individuals concerned felt their hurt deeply, and it caused them spiritual problems. But the Lord brought them all through these experiences, if not unscarred, certainly with a stronger faith than ever. And they each testify to how greatly they were helped by the prayers and comfort of fellow Christians.

The Bible teaches that tribulation and suffering is something the Christian must expect in this world. The night before Calvary, Jesus Christ said: 'In this world you will have trouble. But take heart! I have overcome the world' (John 16:33). Going on to the book of Acts, we find that this is also what the apostles taught. In Acts 14, for instance, we find the apostle Paul going back to the churches he had established on his first missionary journey. He wants to strengthen and encourage them, but he tells them, 'We must go through many hardships to enter the kingdom of God' (v.22). Trials, problems and sufferings, then, are not to surprise the Christian: rather, the lack of them would be surprising! The question is, How do we deal with these things?

The usual effect of tribulation upon an unbeliever is to make him bitter. Suffering often causes the nominal churchgoer to feel sorry for himself and to blame God. But, says Paul, the reaction of the true Christian—the person justified by faith—is to '*rejoice* in . . . sufferings' (Rom. 5:3). How can we rejoice in affliction, illness, pressures, difficulties, persecutions? If Paul had told us to put up with them without too much grumbling, we could perhaps understand. But no, the apostle is much more positive than that: what he tells us to do is to rejoice. And this is the consistent teaching of Scripture. The Lord Jesus Himself said, 'Blessed are you when people insult you, persecute you and falsely say all kinds of evil against you because of me. Rejoice and be glad, because great is your reward in heaven' (Matt. 5:11-12). In the book of Acts we see this actually worked out in the experience of the apostles. Peter and John had been flogged, but they rejoiced 'because they had been counted worthy of suffering disgrace for the Name' (Acts 5:41).

Admittedly, the verses we have quoted refer particularly to suffering that arises from persecution and not from sickness; but, whatever the cause of our troubles, the basic principle remains the same. In many ways, suffering that arises from persecution is easier to bear, for at least the Christian can understand its source, and the reason why it occurs. But all too often the Christian who faces sorrow or illness does not know why these things have happened, and this can cause him greater spiritual problems.

What does it mean to 'rejoice in sufferings'? It certainly does not mean that the Christian *enjoys* suffering. We are not meant to be morbid oddities who take pleasure in pain. When troubles come our way, our immediate reaction is not rejoicing, but perplexity and grief. That is not wrong, but the Christian does not stop there.

The reaction of the Christian to tribulations is not an automatic one. It is not a case of 'Come what may, I'm always happy.' He is enabled to glory in them as the result of the application of his faith. Because he is a man of faith he is able to do certain things.

D. M. Lloyd-Jones

'I consider that our present sufferings are not worth comparing with the glory that will be revealed in us.'

—Romans 8:18

1. The Christian's approach to suffering

THE Bible is a very practical book, touching on every facet of life. It therefore has much to say on the problem of suffering, not only facing up to its reality, but also indicating how we should approach it. Both by direct teaching and also by example, we are shown that there are basically two ways in which the Christian can approach suffering. We shall call them the positive and negative approach.

The positive approach

The positive approach to the problem of suffering is expressed very clearly by the apostle Paul in Romans 5:3,4—'Not only so, but we also rejoice in our sufferings, because we know that suffering produces perseverance; perseverance, character; and character, hope.'

This is not a matter of will power or temperament. If it were merely that, it would have no spiritual content. What Paul is referring to is not something that is true of you if you have a special sort of disposition, but rather something common to every child of God, irrespective of temperament. This rejoicing is possible because of what we *know*—and it is something known only to Christians. We know that God in Christ has displayed an amazing love for us. We know that our salvation is not something we deserve but is all of His grace. We know that the Lord has kept us and will not allow us to lose the precious gift of salvation. And because of what we know of the love and grace of God, we are aware that suffering is not a totally destructive, meaningless experience, but it even produces certain benefits: 'suffering produces perseverance, ... character, ... hope.'

We may be going through life without too much trouble, and since everything seems to be going well for us, we can become casual in our faith and rather prone to take things for granted. Then some severe trial comes. At first it bewilders

7

us; we begin to waver, but because we are Christians we cry to the Lord, realizing as never before how weak we are, and how dependent upon our heavenly Father. The problem causes us to pray with greater intensity and urgency than ever before. We are being taught to wait on the Lord; we are being taught to endure, to *persevere.* It is a sad confession, but all too often perseverance is only learnt in times of trial and tribulation.

Perseverance in turn will develop Christian *character.* The fact that we do not sink beneath the waves of sorrow will strengthen our resolve to lean more upon the Lord. Our assurance of His love is deepened, and our total character as a Christian matures. This will inevitably produce a stronger *hope.*

Notice how Paul has now gone full circle. In verse 2 he was rejoicing in hope of the glory of God. But then these trials intervened. They seem so purposeless and appear to deny the hope of glory; but on the contrary they serve to bring us back to that hope, and they make us much more aware of our God and our salvation than we ever were before. We should not be surprised to discover that one of the most effective means of strengthening assurance is suffering. That is what the Scriptures teach, and it is confirmed in our experience. The most severe trials can cause us great distress and even put our faith under intense pressure, but the end-product will be a greater love for God and a deeper assurance of salvation. We do not want tribulations; we do not like suffering; but as Christians we cannot but agree with Psalm 119:71—'It was good for me to be afflicted so that I might learn your decrees.'

This is the positive, biblical way to approach suffering, but it does not come automatically. In our sad experiences, even though we are Christians, we can wallow in self-pity and give in at the slightest pressure. Whilst we adopt that attitude, there will be no perseverance, no deepening of character, and a greatly diminished hope. The right way is to face the problems, knowing that we are not going to enjoy them in the flesh, but determining that as long as they are there we will use the time and experience to draw nearer to God. Of course we must seek to get rid of the troubles. If the problem is

8

sickness, we must seek medical help. If it is a spiritual problem, we turn to God's servants for the Lord to minister to us through them. If it is friction and quarrels, we seek the biblical remedy. But in the meantime we must not allow the problems to destroy our relationship with God; they must be used not as gravestones, but as stepping-stones to Him. Only then will we be able to rejoice in suffering.

The negative approach

The negative approach to suffering is embodied in the question, 'Why?' In this context the question is always a destructive one because it contains within it an accusation against the love and mercy of God—Why should God allow this to happen to me? What have I done to deserve such sorrow and pain? For the Christian to begin to think in this way only aggravates the problem. Such questioning soon leads to bitterness and self-pity. Instead of knowing the promised peace of God in our troubles, God is shut out and the pain and anguish are multiplied.

There is no answer to the question 'Why?' To such a towering problem as the suffering of men and women the Bible nowhere attempts to give glib, superficial answers. We know that suffering in general, pain, disease, and sorrow, are all the result of sin's invasion of God's creation. God will deal with this one day, and there will be a new heaven and a new earth, with no sin, and consequently with no sorrow or pain, no tears or grief. But to argue from the general to the particular, and claim that each case of suffering is a result of that individual's personal sin, is a view that finds no support or sympathy in the Bible. In John 9:1-3 and Luke 13:1-5 Jesus Christ refuted such callous nonsense very firmly.

Just as suffering is not the direct result of personal guilt, so also personal righteousness does not makes us immune from suffering. To ask, 'Why should God allow this to happen to me?' implies that I have done nothing to deserve my painful experience. That may well be true, but it is irrelevant. The whole approach to the problem embodied in the question 'Why?' is negative and unproductive. It is probably quite natural and understandable, for we all ask it in times of great stress, but it does not help. What we should be asking is not 'Why?' but 'How?' How can I as a Christian learn more of

9

God in this experience? How can I glorify God in my suffering? This may not be the most natural response, but it is undoubtedly the most helpful, and in the long run the most comforting.

A biblical example

The negative approach is exemplified very clearly in the book of Job. The moral and spiritual character of Job is revealed to us in the very first verse: 'This man was blameless and upright; he feared God and shunned evil.' So whatever follows is obviously not a direct result of Job's sin. What happened is related in the remainder of chapter one: he loses everything that is precious to him, and it is the activity of Satan that causes the calamity (vv.6-12). 'We are reminded that beyond the world we see, there is an invisible realm where spiritual forces are at work, whose influence upon the course of human history and of individual lives is beyond our full comprehension' (Herbert Carson).

Job's reaction to this invasion of sorrow and anguish is what you might expect from such a godly man: 'he fell to the ground in worship and said: ''Naked I came from my mother's womb, and naked I shall depart. The Lord gave and the Lord has taken away; may the name of the Lord be praised.'' In all this, Job did not sin by charging God with wrongdoing' (vv.20,21). This is highly commendable, but it is an attitude that is soon put under intense pressure.

The situation is further aggravated when Job's own body is afflicted 'with painful sores from the soles of his feet to the top of his head.' This new affliction draws forth from his wife the bitter advice, 'Curse God and die!' This is the normal reaction of sinful men and women: blame God. 'Where is your God now?', they challenge the believer; and in a situation of great pain and deep sorrow their words can appear plausible to him. The pressure is mounting, but Job does not waver yet. 'He replied, ''You are talking like a foolish woman. Shall we accept good from God, and not trouble?'' In all this, Job did not sin in what he said' (2:10).

There is no doubt about it, Job is a most remarkable man; but even such a man bends under continued pressure. Three friends arrive to comfort him. They come with the best of intentions and they speak a great deal of truth, but because their basic understanding of the problem of suffering is false, they nearly succeed in destroying Job. Before the friends even speak, this man of God is beginning to lose control of himself. 'Job ... cursed the day of his birth. He said ... "I have no peace, no quietness; I have no rest, but only turmoil." ' (3:1,26). While he is in such a frame of mind, the brutal coldness of the three comforters' concept of suffering is devastating. They are convinced that it is his own fault, because they take the view that all suffering is the direct result of personal sin (4:7; 8:4).

Job protests strongly against this untenable viewpoint, for he is not aware of any secret sin that could account for the terrible experiences he is facing. But the present sorrow and pain, coupled now with criticism and accusation, are beginning to tell upon him. He protests, 'God has wronged me' (19:6). He cries, 'Have pity on me, my friends, have pity, for the hand of God has struck me' (19:21). We can see how wrong Job is, but we are in no position to criticize him, for all too often we too are overwhelmed with bitterness and self-pity. It is the worst possible frame of mind to be in, because it dishonours God and only adds to our pain. Yet, even in the darkness of chapter 19, there is a glimmer of light. 'I know that my Redeemer lives, and that in the end he will stand upon the earth. And after my skin has been destroyed, yet in my flesh I will see God' (vv.25,26). Our loving Father will not let us fall completely. David's experience was similar in Psalm 73: 'But as for me, my feet had almost slipped; I had nearly lost my foothold ... When my heart was grieved and my spirit embittered, I was senseless and ignorant; I was a brute beast before you. Yet I am always with you; you hold me by my right hand' (vv.2,21-23). Ultimately Job comes to the place where he makes the same confession as David: 'Surely I spoke of things I did not understand, things too wonderful for me to know' (42:3). All accusations against God are groundless, and what we say in bitterness and self-pity eventually has to be repented of.

Job still has some way to go, however, before he arrives at that point, and one further attitude has to be considered. A young man by the name of Elihu speaks (chapters 32-37).

This man has a great concept of God: 'How great is God—beyond our understanding!' (36:26). Suffering, argues Elihu, has a purpose: 'God does all these things to a man ... to turn back his soul from the pit, that the light of life may shine on him' (33:29,30). In other words, God uses suffering as a means of discipline which works ultimately for our benefit: 'those who suffer he delivers in their suffering; he speaks to them in their affliction' (36:15). This is an answer that finds support in the New Testament (Heb. 12:6; 1 Peter 1:6,7), but it is not the only answer.

The final and complete biblical answer to the vexed question of suffering is one that is only intelligible and acceptable to a man of faith. In the last four chapters of Job, God Himself speaks. It is a marvellous description of the might and majesty of God, but 'You will observe that God has not answered his questions, He has not solved the problem. He has not unlocked the mystery of suffering. He has simply revealed Himself as a God of power and wisdom and love, and asked for Job's trust. God is concerned rather to arouse our faith than to satisfy our curiosity' (John Stott). This would not satisfy an unbeliever, but to a man of faith like Job it is more than enough. The bitterness and self-pity evaporate before the goodness and greatness of God, to be replaced by humility and repentance (42:1-6). Not repentance for some secret sin that may have caused all the trouble, but repentance for sin in the trouble. Once more he is at peace with God; once more he is aware of the presence of God. He surrenders to God's will, and his experience of God is now deeper than it has ever been before, 'My ears had heard of you but now my eyes have seen you' (42:5).

> What then is the message of the book of Job? It is this. When faced with calamity or stricken with sickness, the mind must be engrossed not in our sickness (for that is morbid self-pity), nor in our sins (for that is introspective self-accusation), but partly in the moral and spiritual profit to be derived from suffering, which is valuable self-discipline, and best of all in God Himself. This is humble self-surrender to the God of power and wisdom and love, who has been fully and finally revealed in the cross. This is the sober, wise realism of Christian worship.
>
> John Stott

2. The promises of God

THE Bible recognizes the fact of the suffering of God's people, and exhorts us: 'do not be surpised at the painful trial you are suffering, as though something strange were happening to you' (1 Peter 4:12). It is true that here the apostle Peter was speaking primarily of the suffering of persecution, but none the less the basic principle holds true. There are many biblical passages in which God promises to be with His people during times of severe sorrow and anguish. Let us consider just one of these promises —

> 'When you pass through the waters, I will be with you; and when you pass through the rivers, they will not sweep over you. When you walk through the fire, you will not be burned; the flames will not set you ablaze' (Isaiah 43:2).

God is here promising that when we have to go through the waters of sorrow or the fires of affliction; when we find ourselves in great difficulties, facing grave problems, pressures and perplexities — 'I will be with you.'

Comfort

Even viewed on its own, this promise is most thrilling and comforting to the Christian; but when seen in its context, it takes on a glory that can only cause us to praise and adore the God of our salvation. The previous chapter concludes with a terrible description of the sin and rebellion of God's people (Isa. 42:20). They had sinned by ignoring the revealed will and purpose of God, with the inevitable result that, 'they would not follow his ways' (v.24). That in turn brings the wrath of God upon them (v.25). You might expect, therefore, that chapter 43 would go on to tell us of the frightening consequences of such a rejection of God, but in fact it is quite the opposite. It is a message of comfort.

This in no way condones the sin, but it is a remarkable evidence of the grace and mercy of the Lord. God's love and care for us is never dependent upon our faithfulness, but upon His own holy character. There are many times in our Christian life when by our actions we seem to forfeit the blessings of God, but in such situations our loving Father surprises us with beautiful tokens of love and care. Such mercies do not cause us to trifle with the grace of God, but quite the opposite: we are humbled and overwhelmed, and our hearts respond with greater and more ardent love to our God and Saviour.

The Promiser

A promise is only as valuable as the one making it. Any fool or liar can make the most glorious promises, but they are either unable or unwilling to fulfil them. In church there may be a pastor, or elders, and many Christian friends who will stand by us in our sorrows and troubles, and this is a great thing. They help us to carry the burden, and as Christians we can thank God for each other. But, over and above that, God Himself promises, 'I will be with you.'

Notice how God is described in this chapter. He is the God of creation (v.1). The God who is before all others, the first cause, the Almighty, the Omnipotent, the Eternal God. Such a God cares for us! He is also the God of history (v.3); the God who moves and influences nations for His people. People today are always looking for some man to use his influence to pull a few strings for them, but how pathetic that is compared to the almighty power of God working on behalf of the Christian! The reference in verse 3 to Cush (Ethiopia) takes us back to 2 Chronicles 14. Asa, the king of Judah, was faced with an enemy far superior to any he could possibly cope with. The situation seemed hopeless. 'Then Asa called to the Lord his God and said, "Lord, there is no-one like you to help the powerless against the mighty. Help us, O Lord our God, for we rely on you, and in your name we have come against this vast army. O Lord, you are our God; do not let man prevail against you' (v.11). The result of that prayer was a great victory for the people of God.

How prone we are as Christians to forget how mighty our God is! Isaiah in chapter 40 has to remind a forgetful people, '"Here is your God!" See, the Sovereign Lord comes with power' (vv.9,10). Why does our God come with power? 'He

14

tends his flock like a shepherd: he gathers the lambs in his arms and carries them close to his heart' (v.11). The purpose of His power is to gather and care for the lambs. Power and gentleness—what a glorious combination!—and it works on our behalf!

Christian, this is the Promiser; this is your God.

Why does God bother?

God tells us in Isaiah 43 why He makes such a glorious promise—'you are mine' (v.1).This statement is amplified in verse 4: 'Since you are precious and honoured in my sight, and because I love you'. These are remarkable statements of warmth, love and affection. Who is it that is precious to God? Surely not I, with all my doubts, fears, and disobedience? Yes, you—if you are a Christian. The promise is not to everyone; it is made to those of whom God says, 'I have redeemed you; I have called you by name' (v.1). In other words, the promise applies to a Christian redeemed by the blood of Jesus, and called by the grace of God from the darkness of sin to the light of salvation. So if you are a Christian, God is promising to be with you in your troubles because you belong to Him, and He cares deeply about you.

How do we claim the promise?

It is a tragic fact that even though our heavenly Father makes such a thrilling promise to us, many Christians go through the waters of sorrow and fires of affliction and seem to know nothing of the presence of God. The fault is not God's; it is ours for failing to claim the promise. How do we make such a promise real in our experience? The answer is that in our troubles we need to remember two things.

First of all, *remember who you are.* You belong to God; you are a Christian, so look for and expect help from God. So often Christians do not do this, and in their problems and trials they act and behave like non-Christians. They grumble, moan, despair and become bitter, and it is all because they have forgotten who they are. They are Christians; they are precious to God; He has redeemed them; He calls them His own. Yet they behave as if there is no one to help them, no Almighty God to care for them.

The Israelites had seen God's almighty power demonstrated on their behalf in redeeming them from the bondage of Egypt. They were now free, redeemed, loved by God and on their way to the Promised Land. Everything was fine, until they encountered their first real problem. Pharaoh had changed his mind about releasing them and was pursuing them with his army to haul them back to slavery. In front of them was the Red Sea; behind them the Egyptians. And what did this redeemed people do? They panicked. Read Exodus 14:10-12. They forgot who they were, and thought that because they were helpless the situation was hopeless. Moses has to remind them very forcefully to be calm: 'Stand firm and you will see the deliverance the Lord will bring you today' (v.13) 'Be still', he urges, 'behave like those who are redeemed, loved by God and precious to Him.' When they do that, God deals with the seemingly hopeless situation.

Our God is a God of His word; He means what He says. That is why in Psalm 23 David was able to say, 'Even though I walk through the valley of the shadow of death, I will fear no evil'. Why not? Because 'you are with me'. He knew the promise and believed it. So then, remember who you are: you are not an ordinary person; you are redeemed, loved, called by God, and precious to Him.

Secondly, *remember who God is,* and do not be afraid to trust Him completely, because He is able. His loving care is matched by His almighty power, and He can uphold us in times of severe distress. The story of Shadrach, Meshach and Abednego in the book of Daniel is a vivid reminder of this. Because of their faithfulness to the Lord they literally had to go into the fire (Daniel 3:19-23). When King Nebuchadnezzar looked into the furnace later, he saw not three figures but four, and the fourth was like the Son of God. 'I will be with you ... when you walk through the fire, you will not be burned.'

But what about those Christians who are not miraculously delivered? Those whose body and mind are racked with the pain of disease, and who finally die, perhaps in agony—how does God's promise apply to them? To answer, let us take another biblical example—Stephen (Acts 7). Stephen was stoned to death. The enemies of God hurled stone after stone

16

upon him, cracked his skull, broke his ribs and bones. It must have been a most painful death, but we read, 'Stephen, full of the Holy Spirit, looked up to heaven and saw the glory of God, and Jesus standing at the right hand of God' (Acts 7:55). The Triune God ministered to this man in his extreme weakness. God was with him.

There is an awful tendency for us to think sometimes that these biblical examples of God's dealings with great men have nothing to do with us. We say, 'That was Stephen, and I am no Stephen.' That does not matter. The promise is not to great, super-spiritual Christians, but to those whom God has redeemed. If you are redeemed, the promise is applicable to you every bit as much as it was to Stephen. The Bible is not a book of meaningless theories, but the Word of the living God. God says, in your troubles and sorrows, 'I will be with you.' Believe that, and look to see God's grace sustaining you, so that even if there is no miraculous deliverance there is the sweet and embracing presence of the God to whom you are precious.

3: Some thoughts from J. C. Ryle

(Excerpts from chapter 14 of *Practical Religion*)

HOW shall we learn to bear sickness patiently, when sickness comes to our turn? We must lay up stores of grace in the time of health. We must seek for the sanctifying influence of the Holy Ghost over our unruly tempers and dispositions. We must make a real business of our prayers, and regularly ask for strength to endure God's will as well as to do it. Such strength is to be had for the asking: 'If ye shall ask any thing in my name, I will do it for you' (John 14:14).

I cannot think it needless to dwell on this point. I believe the passive graces of Christianity receive far less notice than they deserve. Meekness, gentleness, long-suffering, faith, patience, are all mentioned in the Word of God as fruits of the Spirit. They are passive graces which specially glorify God. They often make men think, who despise the active side of the Christian character. Never do these graces shine so brightly as they do in the sick-room. They enable many a sick person to preach a silent sermon, which those around him never forget. Would you adorn the doctrine you profess? Would you make your Christianity beautiful in the eyes of others? Then take the hint I give you this day. Lay up a store of patience against the time of illness. Then, though your sickness be not to death, it shall be for the 'glory of God' (John 11:4) . . .

I exhort all true Christians . . . to remember how much they may glorify God in the time of sickness, and to *lie quiet in God's hand when they are ill*.

I feel it very important to touch on this point. I know how ready the heart of a believer is to faint, and how busy Satan is in suggesting doubts and questionings, when the body of a Christian is weak. I have seen something of the depression and melancholy which sometimes comes upon the children of God when they are suddenly laid aside by disease, and obliged to sit still. I have marked how prone some good people are to torment themselves with morbid thoughts at such seasons, and to say in their hearts, 'God has forsaken me: I am cast out of His sight.'

I earnestly entreat all sick believers to remember that they may honour God as much by patient suffering as they can by active work. It often shows more grace to sit still than it does to go to and fro, and perform great exploits. I entreat them to remember that Christ cares for them as much when they are sick as He does when they are well, and that the very chastisement they feel so acutely is sent in love, and not in anger. Above all, I entreat them to recollect the sympathy of Jesus for all His weak members. They are always tenderly cared for by Him, but never so much as in their time of need. Christ has had great experience of sickness. He knows the heart of a sick man. He used to see 'all manner of sickness, and all manner of disease' when He was upon earth. He felt specially for the sick in the days of His flesh. He feels for them specially still. Sickness and suffering, I often think, make believers more like their Lord in experience, than health. 'Himself took our infirmities, and bare our sicknesses' (Matt. 8:17). The Lord Jesus was a 'man of sorrows, and acquainted with grief' (Isa. 53:3). None have such an opportunity of learning the mind of a suffering Saviour as suffering disciples . . .

The day may come when, after a long fight with disease, we shall feel that medicine can do no more, and that nothing remains but to die. Friends will be standing by, unable to help us. Hearing, eyesight, even the power of praying, will be fast failing us. The world and its shadows will be melting beneath our feet. Eternity, with its realities, will be looming large before our minds. What shall support us in that trying hour? What shall enable us to feel, 'I fear no evil' (Psalm 23:4)? Nothing, nothing can do it but close communion with Christ. Christ dwelling in our hearts by faith,—Christ putting His right arm under our heads . . . Christ can alone give us the complete victory in the last struggle.

Let us cleave to Christ more closely, love Him more heartily, live to Him more thoroughly, copy Him more exactly, confess Him more boldly, follow Him more fully. Religion like this will always bring its own reward. Worldly people may laugh at it. Weak brethren may think it extreme. But it will wear well . . . In sickness it will bring us peace. In the world to come it will give us a crown of glory that fadeth not away.

PERSONAL TESTIMONIES

We have sought to see something of the biblical teaching on this most vexing problem. But the problem is so personal and the hurt felt is so deep that even with the rich practical help of the Scriptures we often feel that the experience is too much for us. How can we possibly cope? In such situations it can be a help to see how other Christians have faced the experiences that threaten to overwhelm us.

The five experiences related in the following chapters cover different types of suffering. The writers are not theorizing or talking glibly. They have known what it is to suffer (and some of them still are suffering); they have felt the anguish, pain, loneliness and sorrow. Their words therefore are not empty platitudes, but simply express how they felt, and how the Lord drew near to them.

1. 'Peace, be still'

ONE Sunday, a family was leaving church after the evening service. The father crossed the road to return the chapel key, while the mother and two children, Christopher aged nine and Susan aged four and a half, waited on the pavement. The road had three lanes, and down the middle lane two cars came speeding towards each other. Neither took evasive action, and in the subsequent trial the Judge told both drivers, 'I have no doubt that this was, on the part of each of you, a disgraceful piece of driving.'

The result was a crash, with one car sent hurtling across the road into the waiting family. Both children were killed and the mother sustained injuries that kept her on crutches for many weeks.

How do Christians cope in such tragic situations?

The mother's experience

Remembrance Sunday for us is not the day when, like most people, we remember those who died for their country, but the day we lost our two precious children. Sunday, November 13th, started out very much like any other Lord's Day. We were always very busily involved in the activities of the church, in Sunday School and at morning and evening services. We can neither of us recall what the sermon was about that evening, but we remember that the last hymn was, 'God is working His purpose out'. Christopher had sat next to me, sharing my Bible and following the reading intently.

As we waited on the pavement there was a terrific collision on the road and one car careered towards us. I myself was knocked out for a while; when I came round I remember shouting frantically to my sister, 'Where are Christopher and Susie?' We could not find them for some time.

How people who have no faith in God manage in a time of crisis I do not know. We prayed there at the roadside amidst all the confusion. How wonderful our heavenly Father is! He is always at hand.

The ambulance seemed to take hours to arrive, and I still cannot enter the casualty department of the hospital without first seeking God's strength in prayer. We were told that Christopher had been dead on arrival and that Susan had died in the theatre. Why, Lord, why should our two precious children be taken from us? They were always so full of life and energy. After having noisy, chattering children, the horrible quiet and the awful emptiness led us just to sit together in absolute despair. The hardest part of that week for me was at the funeral, seeing those two small coffins and knowing that I would never hold my children in my arms again and tell them I loved them. Still, the funeral was a very uplifting service.

Those first few days and weeks after the accident were very difficult. All we seemed to want to do was to spend hours in prayer together. Darkness and bedtime I used to dread. Satan would keep me awake, even after taking sleeping tablets, wondering if the children had suffered. I was grateful for Christian friends who dropped in and spent time in prayer with me.

I found it very difficult to enter the children's bedrooms, and only after much prayer did I feel able to do so. There facing me on Christopher's desk was his last colouring picture from Sunday school. It was the scene of Jesus with His disciples in the boat in the storm. Underneath in Christopher's bold writing were the words, 'Peace, be still.' I felt this was surely a message telling me to be assured that my children were at peace and safe in the arms of Jesus. From that day, confidently trusting the Saviour, I discontinued my sleeping tablets, telling Satan to flee.

The next month, Christmas, was very lonely. Time does heal, though. God gave us strength to continue, and in His mercy He gave us two more children, a son and a daughter. What a wonderful Saviour is ours, ordering our lives so that the trial of our faith, 'being much more precious than of gold that perisheth, though it be tried with fire, might be found unto praise and honour and glory at the appearing of Jesus Christ' (1 Pet. 1:7). Unto our Saviour be all the glory!

The father's experience

I had taken the keys back to where they were kept and was walking along the pavement when the two cars collided. I rushed those last few paces, knowing that my family was standing right in the path of the car. I searched frantically in the wreckage and called out. I heard my wife calling. Chris was under one side of the car and Sue the other side. There was lots of activity and everything seemed to be chaos. I prayed and prayed. How we prayed in those minutes on the roadside!

The ambulance seemed to be hours in coming, but when it did arrive the ambulance men were good and efficient and sought to comfort us. In the hospital casualty department the doctor told us the children were dead, and despair was at its deepest. Surely the Lord had not let this happen! It was as if the end of everything had come, and we even felt at that time that death would be the acceptable way out for us.

Identifying the children at the hospital was a very lonely experience. My wife stayed at home and the police drove me in. I remember, as I looked at those two little bodies, that it was as if the devil was saying to me, 'This is final, absolutely final. There is no hope now.' But our hope is fixed in Christ, and I am sure that one day we shall be united with our little ones again, and with the host on high we shall sing before His throne together.

The next few days we were greatly encouraged by the fellowship of Christian friends. They comforted us in our distress and prayed with us in our time of need, and we felt the power of their prayers in that difficult period. We found that truly the grace of our Lord Jesus Christ was sufficient. Although we felt weak and faltered much, we determined we would witness to our faith and trust in our Saviour. And to this end I remember requesting that the gospel should be preached at the funeral. Although our grief was present, we ourselves were uplifted at the funeral service by the preaching of the gospel.

After the funeral I was relieved when the many family members and friends who were not Christians had gone home. I love them, but their words were so empty and their grief without hope. That may sound a little uncharitable, but we both felt that the Lord's people were closer to us and we looked forward to seeing them first of all. We cannot always understand the ways of the Lord, so we just have to wait for that day when we see Him face to face—things will be clear then. I only praise God that He spared my dear wife on that night and we can rejoice in Him together, for we know whom we have believed and He is 'able to keep that which we have committed unto him against that day' when we will meet them in glory.

In retrospect

Looking back over the past years, it is still difficult for us to understand why the Lord allowed this event in our lives which brought us so much heartache. One thing we know is that Satan was always around to cast doubt on our faith in Christ our Lord. But He is the Sovereign God and His purpose will be done, and surely this will be for our own good in the end. His grace is sufficient for the greatest need, and although the pain of our loss is never far away, we praise God for Timothy and Amanda who were born in later years. Through them the Lord has brought a new joy into our lives.

> *Does Jesus care when I've said 'Good-bye!'*
> *To the dearest on earth to me,*
> *And my sad heart aches*
> *Till it nearly breaks:*
> *Is this aught to Him?—does He see?*
>
> *Oh yes, He cares! I know He cares,*
> *His heart is touched with my grief;*
> *When the days are weary,*
> *The long nights dreary,*
> *I know my Saviour cares!*

2. God does not make mistakes

THE night before my husband was to undergo his second heart operation, I said to my mother on the telephone, 'Whatever the outcome, God does not make mistakes.' Three days later I had to prove that I really believed this, as my husband died, never having regained consciousness.

My immediate thoughts were for my three daughters, especially the youngest who was only seven. I was thinking aloud while with a doctor and sister in the Intensive Care Unit, and said 'How can I tell my daughters? But God will help me.' As soon as I said that, the doctor said to the sister, 'She will be all right.' He obviously knew where I would get my strength from.

I telephoned my brother who lived about fifty miles away, and within two or three hours he and my mother were with us. They were a great support to us, as were the many friends within our churches, and our other relations. I do thank God for them all. During the early days I had a calmness and peace which enabled me to do the necessary things and make needful decisions. I knew that my husband's work was completed, as God would otherwise have intervened.

My husband was a minister in one of the denominations, the house and furniture being provided with the appointment. This meant that we would need to find accommodation and furniture. We were not living near any of our relations, but one of my sisters and her husband very kindly suggested that we could stay with them until we had time to decide what we wished to do. We needed to leave the manse for another minister to take over; also my daughters' education had to be taken into consideration. After thinking and praying about this, we left the manse and went to my sister's home.

The denomination we were in agreed to buy a house for us, and we would pay rent for it. We were to look for suitable property and get in touch with headquarters. There were not many houses for sale at that time. After looking at several which were not suitable, I called on a Christian couple who had lived with my mother at one time. They were about to go abroad and intended letting their house furnished. I suggested to them that if they were to consider selling, we could come to an arrangement to buy the contents of the house. I left them to think and pray about it, and two days later they had decided to sell. It was a real answer to prayer. God was meeting our needs fully.

After moving into this house, I went through a time of feeling very alone, although I had my daughters with me. I had previously not spent much time thinking about heaven, but during this period I did, and longed to be there, knowing full well it was not in my hands. Although God had so wonderfully provided for us, I began to feel sorry for myself, until one day I went down with 'flu. Then it came home to me what my responsibilities were to my daughters. They still needed a mother's care and guidance, and God had promised never to leave us or forsake us, whatever our situation, so I claimed this promise for the days ahead.

Since our move we had been attending an evangelical church, to which my family belonged, more than the denominational church. As I thought of my daughters, I wanted more than anything that they would *all* come to know the Lord. (My eldest daughter was a believer.) I prayed that I would do what was right before God. Not having their father to guide them, I felt that more than ever they would need consistent teaching. So, although it was not easy, after many years in the denomination we left and joined the evangelical church. Since then my other two daughters have come to know the Lord, and I know that they value the teaching which they had in the early years of their Christian lives.

Some months after my husband's death, one of my daughters went through a very difficult time. My doctor was very helpful, and in conversation he made the point that I should not be afraid to let my daughter see that I needed to cry. She was bottling up her feelings, and probably thinking that if I did not show that I was upset, then neither should she. After talking things over with her, and answering numerous questions, I found that she settled down normally.

26

My need for permanent employment was something I now had to face. I had various temporary jobs. My applications for permanent posts were many, but though I had interviews I did not get the posts. These occasions were very demoralizing. It is easy to sit in church listening to helpful sermons, but not so easy to put into practice what they teach; only by constantly drawing on God's grace is it at all possible. The post that I was eventually to get was more suitable than the others I had applied for, and if I had gained any of the previous posts, by now I would have been made redundant. God does not make mistakes.

In a letter that my husband left for me, he gave me two texts: Isaiah 40:31—'But those who hope in the Lord will renew their strength. They will soar on wings like eagles; they will run and not grow weary, they will walk and not be faint'; and Isaiah 41:10—'So do not fear, for I am with you; do not be dismayed, for I am your God. I will strengthen you and help you; I will uphold you with my righteous right hand.'

Ten years later I am writing this, having proved the truth of those Scriptures in many situations. It has not been easy. On many occasions I felt that the practicalities of everyday living and making decisions were difficult. There were many times when I became fearful and over-anxious, particularly in things affecting my daughters, and then my spiritual life would be affected. But the Lord has been very patient with me; He would remind me that He had promised to strengthen and uphold me. I do not fully understand, as yet, the ways the Lord leads, but I do thank Him for giving me the assurance that *He is* in control, and I need not be afraid. I know that nothing will ever be able to separate me from the love of God that is in Christ Jesus my Lord.

All I have needed Thy hand hath provided—
'Great is Thy faithfulness', Lord, unto me!

3. Strength in weakness

GOD was very good and gracious to the whole of my family, especially to me. From early childhood we were taught the Scriptures, and eventually, in later years, the Lord saved all nine of my parents' children. Not only was the Lord's hand known in spiritual blessings, but He blessed me physically in a wonderful way. I had an extremely strong body, being able, at the age of 17, to carry quite easily 2¼ cwt. sacks of wheat all day long, and even 3¼ cwt. at times.

For the first 15½ years of my life I was a little horror, having one of the worst tempers imaginable, and being positively dangerous when upset by anyone. In January 1936 the Lord gloriously saved me, and after that everything was different. Even the fields in which I had worked for years were different; so were the trees, hedges and flowers. Ploughing with a team of horses became a pleasure rather than a drudgery. God was seen everywhere, and in everything. It was really true that

> *Something lives in every hue*
> *Christless eyes have never seen.*

Now that the Lord Jesus Christ had become my Saviour, the great Creator and Sustainer of all things had become very, very real to me. He gave me a desire to tell everyone of His love.

I married and had a dairy farm on which I worked for several years practically on my own. I had to work very hard, but the Lord blessed in a wonderful way, granting much increase. Although I was never well off materially, things tended to take a place they should not have. I soon found that the broken cisterns of material possessions did not satisfy the deep yearnings of my soul.

When about 40 years old, I had a serious illness and was in hospital for three weeks. I lost two stones in weight, and it was said that I would not be able to work again. Our farm, being intensive dairying and intensive poultry, was extremely

28

hard work, and it seemed that the only answer would be to acquire a much larger farm, and change to 'dog and stick' farming, which was much easier. This seemed almost impossible, but we prayed about the matter, and after a few weeks I had a telephone call from the owner of an estate, whom I had never met or spoken to before. He offered me the tenancy of a 260-acre farm which, after seeing, I accepted, believing that the Lord was leading in this. One cannot but ask, Why such favour to me, of all men?

After many years of good health, I have found that the last two or three years have in many ways been the most difficult —for the following reasons:

1) I experience continued bodily weakness. I now suffer from diabetes, angina, and sideroblastic anaemia. This last problem means that my bone marrow does not produce the necessary red cells. Because of this I have to enter hospital every five weeks to receive a transfusion of six units of blood. Over the last two years I have had fifteen such transfusions.

2) A side-effect of this has been that my eyesight is now so poor that I cannot read. I miss tremendously the simple pleasure of being able to read God's Word and expositions of Scripture.

3) The work on the farm, which I have been used to doing and loved, I am now unable to do. Before my son, Michael, was old enough to relieve me, I was accustomed to not going to bed for a period of three to five weeks at lambing time. I really loved the work and caring for the sheep, and was not abnormally tired after such an effort.

4) The most important difficulty of all has been that I am an elder of my church, and have certain pastoral responsibilities which I have been unable to fulfil. I have felt very guilty when meeting those in the church for whom I am responsible, having been unable to visit for a long time. I love to be able to serve my fellow-believers in some small way. All this has caused me very much frustration, and at times depression.

Then came a time when I had to miss seven Sundays of worship. These, and fellowship with the brethren, I missed terribly. On the Sunday when I returned, I was overwhelmed by the fact that so many said they had missed me and were glad to see me back. It was not just the number that said so, but what reached my very soul was the reality which I knew was there. One brother told me, 'I'm so glad to see you back—you know, we love you very much.' I could not answer a word, it reached the inner depths of my soul. As I lay on my bed that night, I could not refrain from thanking and praising the Lord for making real to me a new dimension of Christian love that I had not known before.

A question I have been asked is, 'Do you feel any bitterness in all this?' Frustration and sometimes depression, yes, but bitterness, 'NO'. How could I be bitter? I am in the hands of the Almighty God, who knows the end from the beginning; who took a sinful ploughboy and gloriously saved him 46 years ago, and who, every day of my life since, has been preparing me for eternity with Himself. Many years ago the Lord gave me a sight of my heart, its blackness and deceitfulness. I have never ceased to be amazed at what God has done for me in Christ. So often my cry has been,

> *Depth of mercy! can there be*
> *Mercy still reserved for me?*
> *Can my God His wrath forbear?*
> *Me, the chief of sinners, spare?*

How could I be bitter towards the One who has kept me, protected and shielded me every day of my life, in spite of my sinfulness, and has so tenderly cared for me?

Many people have told me that they are praying that the Lord will heal me. That is another thing that has amazed me—how many there are who are praying for me. If the Lord chooses to heal me, I shall praise Him for it, but I have not asked Him to do so. I am very grateful to everyone who prays for my healing, but I view it like this: I am in God's hands, and it would not surprise me if He did strengthen me so that I might go on longer than I believe at the moment is possible; but if He chooses not to do so, then perhaps it won't be very long before I go to Glory.

One thing has stood out in this illness of mine, and it is how the Lord has used His people's love and concern to encourage me. Until recently I did not appreciate how important this is. I never fully realized what Christian love should be, and how we should feel for one another.

The only safe place to rest, I find, is in the promises of our God. 'Thou wilt keep him in perfect peace, whose mind is stayed on thee' (Isaiah 26:3).

> *Stayed upon Jehovah,*
> *Hearts are fully blessed,*
> *Finding, as He promised,*
> *Perfect peace and rest.*

(Since this testimony was written, our brother has entered his Lord's presence).

4. 'He giveth more grace'

HAVING known what it is to suffer physically, mentally and emotionally, I can but look back to the beginning and ask what God has taught me in it all. Primarily, I think, He taught me that I had no personal relationship with Him, and that if ever I were to enjoy Him and His blessings I must first be acceptable in His sight. I first came to a realization of this need when I was being treated by a psychiatrist for puerperal depression. It suddenly dawned on me during my course of treatment that I was putting the psychiatrist in God's place, so I refused any further treatment at that point and my search began.

A Christian friend gave me a book called *Woman to Woman,* which compares what a woman is without Jesus Christ and what she can be with Him. This brought to light many shortcomings and made a marked impression on me—an impression further deepened by the teaching of my present church. Previously I had been a churchgoer and was satisfied with my own respectability. In other words, my view of sin had been man-centred: having never before compared myself with God, I had had no sense of being unable to please Him. I was just doing my best, suppressing my conscience by helping others—until I discovered that all my righteousness is as filthy rags in His sight. What a revelation it was to discover that I hadn't really accepted Jesus' death on the cross as a sufficient sacrifice for me! In my ignorance I had been trying to earn God's approval in my own way, while at the same time completely rejecting His grace. Oh, the blindness of it all! And when I think that, but for God showing me my error, I would have continued on the way that leads to destruction and hell! Thankfully I have repented of my sin and entered into a living relationship with Jesus.

When I first started out on the Christian road I was quite ignorant of what was involved in the battles with the world, the flesh and the devil. God was determined to have His way with me, however, and there have been, and still are, many rough edges to deal with. For example, by nature I am fairly intelligent, strong-minded and independent (proud!), so before I was a Christian I had emigrated to Australia with a view to improving my family's lot. This came about because, when my eldest son was not quite two and my daughter only six weeks old, I had contracted rheumatoid arthritis and coping with toddlers became an almost impossible task. Consequently, since my husband was due to go to Australia on an extended business trip, we decided to emigrate. For four years the arthritis was more or less at bay, but for family reasons we had to abandon that possibility and return to England. I was often frustrated and very disappointed when on my return I quickly fell victim to the ravages of the illness. Indeed it took several years of battling with myself before I realized how wrong I was. It was while listening to a series of addresses on the prophecy of Jonah at the Evangelical Movement of Wales Annual Conference at Aberystwyth that I reached the conclusion that I was just like Jonah: I still really only wanted my will and not God's.

Because Australia was the only place where I had known physical relief since my illness began, it had a very strong pull on me. At the invitation of a Christian friend I even spent a holiday there, but I couldn't stay there with my family over here. I just had to realise that the Lord wanted me to love Him more than my health. Health had always seemed such a legitimate reason for having one's own way; but then, I suppose, so is loving one's family—and still Jesus said: 'If any man come to me, and hate not his father, and mother, and wife, and children, and brethren, and sisters, yea, and his own life also, he cannot be my disciple' (Luke 14:26).

In Aberystwyth, through the story of Jonah, the Lord taught me how wrong I had been in wanting to run off in another direction when He wanted me here. In one of his addresses Dr. Sinclair Ferguson spoke of a woman who said that some of his preaching had made her feel as though her whole life was being dealt with. That too was my experience, and no doubt it will continue to be so, as God has promised to complete the work that He starts within us.

Before I left for the holiday in Australia many prayers had been offered for revival in our church. I too had asked the Lord to revive me, and I'm sure that I had no idea of what the consequences might be. There was a stage when I was aware of sin, but not in depth. I believe I was learning more about this gradually, but I felt, and still feel, that the answer to my prayer came when I discovered Newton's hymn, 'I asked the Lord that I might grow'. The fourth and fifth verses were very real to me:

> *Instead of this, He made me feel*
> *The hidden evils of my heart,*
> *And let the angry powers of hell*
> *Assault my soul in every part.*

> *Yea, more, with His own hand He seemed*
> *Intent to aggravate my woe,*
> *Crossed all the fair designs I schemed,*
> *Blasted my gourds, and laid me low.*

Two years later my mind finally decided that it was overtired through pain and lack of sleep and all my senseless striving. I was reduced to being unable to put my thoughts together and it was very difficult to communicate. I was heart-broken, and yet in those circumstances I knew the Lord's comfort in a very personal way.

In fact, when my mind didn't work, the Holy Spirit brought Scripture to me to comfort me. For this reason Isaiah 43:2 has become very precious to me: 'When thou passest through the waters, I will be with thee; and through the rivers, they shall not overflow thee: when thou walkest through the fire, thou shalt not be burned; neither shall the flame kindle upon thee.' In desperate times I have cried to the Lord and He has answered me with 'I will never leave thee, nor forsake thee' (Hebrews 13:5) and 'Ye are of more value than many sparrows' (Luke 12:7). I have known, too, the Lord sending His people to me with a word from Him at exactly the right time. What a joy it is to open the Bible, knowing that it is possible to meet with the God of all comfort and One who loves us so much that He will not leave us to our own devices!

At this time my utter helplessness was very apparent. However, after being encouraged to give thanks to the Lord when I didn't feel like it, I re-read Roy Hession's book *We Would See Jesus.* Here again I saw Jesus as everything that I am not, and my joy was restored. I was at last learning the sufficiency of God's grace to meet my particular need. And what a surprise I had when I discovered that my favourite hymn, 'He giveth more grace', was written by someone suffering from rheumatoid arthritis! Previously I had been under the mistaken impression that the responsibility for being cheerful rested entirely upon me. What a relief to realize that Christian joy is more than that. In fact, it is no more nor less than giving of thanks and praise to Jesus who has loved us and washed us from sin, and to our heavenly Father who planned a complete salvation for us.

It is a privilege to share in a variety of suffering and to be able to relate to others through it. Is it surprising that, having been set free from sin (though not perfect) and made aware that God is in control, 2 Corinthians 1:3-5 and Romans 8:28 mean so much to me? God has His purpose in all these experiences, and they are both humbling and enriching when we submit, even though we are often perplexed. It is His glory, after all, and we must be content to be His vessels. I have reached the conclusion that I had no right to resist, for the Lord knows the way that I take, and

> *Blessings abound where'er He reigns:*
> *The prisoner leaps to lose his chains;*
> *The weary find eternal rest,*
> *And all the sons of want are blest.*

5. A special little girl

WHEN our second daughter, Dawn, was born almost twelve years ago, she appeared to be a normal, healthy baby. However, as time went by it was obvious to us that she was having convulsions. Our own doctor, when consulted, insisted that they were only wind spasms, but when he persisted he referred her, at the age of fourteen weeks, to the paediatrician at the local hospital, who admitted her to the hospital for tests. As a result of these tests we were told that her brain was damaged, either before or after birth, owing to lack of oxygen, and that she was mentally retarded. Our first reaction was that we could not believe the doctor's diagnosis; then came the question 'Why should God allow this to happen to us?'

The mother's experience

I had no answer to this question for several years, during which time I felt as if my world had crashed around me. Not knowing the exact cause of her brain damage I tortured myself seeking to know if it was something I had done that had caused it. I was angry against God, asking why we should have had a less than perfect child when all our friends were having normal healthy children. I even got to the point of querying His existence if He could allow this to happen to us, and for a time became very bitter towards Him and everyone else as well. I knew a deep despair, and a feeling at times that I wanted to run away and leave everything behind. But God, in His love, patience and long-suffering towards me, showed me that all life comes from Him. I came to understand more of the love of a Sovereign God, and learned to say with Abraham 'Shall not the Judge of all the earth do right?' (Gen. 18:25). In the light of His greatness, who was I to query His dealings with me? There was nothing so special about me to exempt me from trouble. I had to humble myself before the Lord and trust in Him alone for all things. I am thankful now

36

that I had this struggle in accepting Dawn, as it has enabled me to have a far greater understanding of those in similar circumstances.

The father's experience

My experience was different from that of my wife, in that, nine years earlier, I had gone through a similar experience of questioning when my brother had been killed in a car accident. I had been brought to the realization that God is sovereign in all things, and although I still did not know the answer to the question 'Why?' I was able to put my trust and faith in God and see that in all aspects of my life as a Christian He was working His purposes out. I was able to accept my daughter as she was, and was given a strong love for her; when tensions were present, I was able to calm her.

God's grace

As time went by we both knew an increasing sense of loneliness and isolation, as people, including Christians, seemed to be afraid of the difficulties and problems of having a mentally handicapped child. One lesson we learned from this, however, was that, although human friends failed us, the Lord never failed and we were caused to lean more and more on Him.

We had wrestled with the Lord for many hours seeking for Him to heal Dawn, but we had to come to realize that this was not His will for her, and that He had a special purpose for her being as she was. However, we were caused a great deal of mental anguish and spiritual agony by Christians with unbiblical views of suffering, who repeatedly told us that if we had more faith our daughter would be healed. Satan persisted in using this to taunt us with lack of faith, telling us it was our fault that she was in the condition she was. But God had given us an assurance in our hearts that He could heal Dawn at any time if He wanted to do so. For her to be healed at this time, however, would have been the easy way out for us, and we learned to face up to the problems rather than seeking the easy solution. His word in 2 Corinthians 12:9 became very real and precious to us—'My grace is sufficient for thee: for my strength is made *perfect* in *weakness*. Most gladly therefore will I rather glory in my infirmities, that the power of Christ may rest upon [or cover] me'.

When Dawn was about two years old her general health began to deteriorate. She became increasingly susceptible to chest infections, which ended with her being rushed into hospital because the infection caused severe convulsions. These lasted for eight to ten days and, according to the doctors, each time she was ill she went to death's door. At these times we experienced great frustration and helplessness, watching Dawn suffer so much and yet being unable to do anything for her. We learned what it meant to pray 'Thy will, not mine, be done', and to accept His will even if it was not what we wanted; in doing this we knew the 'peace of God, which passeth all understanding', keeping our hearts and minds in Christ Jesus (Philippians 4:7).

The constant convulsions increased brain damage, so that each time we brought her home she needed more attention and patience to stimulate her both mentally and physically. As her mother I knew a physical tiredness that I have never experienced either before her birth or since her death. But God moved in a mysterious way to give me much needed rest. When she was about two and a half years old, I developed eye trouble, which was first of all diagnosed as conjunctivitis but later, correctly, as an ulcer on the cornea of my eye. Every time this flared up I knew intense pain and an inability to open my eyes, and I was forced to spend at least two days in bed while it healed up. As a result of this I was physically rested so as to face once more the task I had to do. My eye was finally operated on and healed eight weeks before Dawn died. The Lord knew that I would no longer need the physical rest.

About five months before she died, Dawn was extremely ill again and in a coma for over four weeks. The doctors could do no more; they stopped giving her antibiotics, saying that it would only be a matter of days, in their opinion, before she died. We saw the Lord's healing hand upon her again in a very remarkable way, for within seven days she was well and at home. The things which are impossible with men are possible with God. After this she made quite a lot of progress: although she could not walk or talk she was much more alert,

38

and during this time she was able to go to the school for mentally handicapped children. She was very responsive to us, and we knew such love for her and thankfulness to the Lord for giving us such a special little girl. By this time she was just over five years old.

It was, therefore, a great shock to us, having left Dawn in a home some miles from our home town whilst we were taking a much needed holiday, to learn that she was once again in hospital, and seriously ill. She died before we were able to get to her, but on learning from the nursing staff that she had died during a convulsion which had not been very pleasant to watch, we can only see again the graciousness of the Lord in sparing us that. Our last memories are of her laughing with us. For a time after her death we felt very guilty, thinking that if we had not left her in the care of strangers she would not have died; but the Lord showed us the truth of Ecclesiastes 3:1,2—'To every thing there is a season, and a time to every purpose under the heaven: a time to be born, and a time to die.' We knew that God in His sovereign will had heard our prayers and healed our daughter completely, and although we were very sad at her passing we did not 'sorrow . . . even as others which have no hope' (1 Thessalonians 4:13).

Looking back over these events from a distance of seven years, the lessons we have learned are that we cannot know all the answers as to why God deals with us in the ways that He does, but as Christians we are sure that He holds our lives in His hands. Whatever happens to us, for good or ill, His way is best and we can safely rest in Him, knowing that He is in control of our lives. To Him be all praise and glory!

We would like to quote a hymn that was brought to our attention the Sunday after the diagnosis was given to us that our daughter was mentally handicapped. It was a tremendous help and encouragement to us through the years, so we sang it at her funeral.

> *Leave God to order all thy ways,*
> *And hope in Him whate'er betide;*
> *Thou'lt find Him in the evil days*
> *Thy all-sufficient strength and guide:*
> *Who trusts in God's unchanging love*
> *Builds on the rock that nought can move.*

Only thy restless heart keep still,
    And wait in cheerful hope, content
To take whate'er His gracious will,
    His all-discerning love, hath sent;
Nor doubt our inmost wants are known
To Him who chose us for His own.

Sing, pray, and swerve not from His ways,
    But do thine own part faithfully;
Trust His rich promises of grace,
    So shall they be fulfilled in thee:
God never yet forsook at need
The soul that trusted Him indeed.